Make a New Friend in Je...

PassAlong Arch® Books help you share Jesus with friends close to you and with children all around the world!

When you've enjoyed this story, pass it along to a friend. When your friend is finished, mail this book to the address below. Concordia Gospel Outreach promises to deliver your book to a boy or girl somewhere in the world to help him or her learn about Jesus.

Myself

My name _____

My address _____

_____

My PassAlong Friend

My name _____

My address _____

_____

When you're ready to give your PassAlong Arch® Book to a new friend who doesn't know about Jesus, mail it to

Concordia Gospel Outreach
3547 Indiana Avenue
St. Louis, MO 63118

PassAlong Series

God's Good Creation
Noah's Floating Zoo
Jesus Stills the Storm
God's Easter Plan

Copyright © 1994 Concordia Publishing House
3558 S. Jefferson Avenue, St. Louis, MO 63118-3968
Manufactured in the United States of America

1 2 3 4 5 6 7 8 9 10   03 02 01 00 99 98 97 96 95 94

God's Good Creation

Genesis 1–2 for Children

Carol Greene
Illustrated by Michelle Dorenkamp

ST. LOUIS

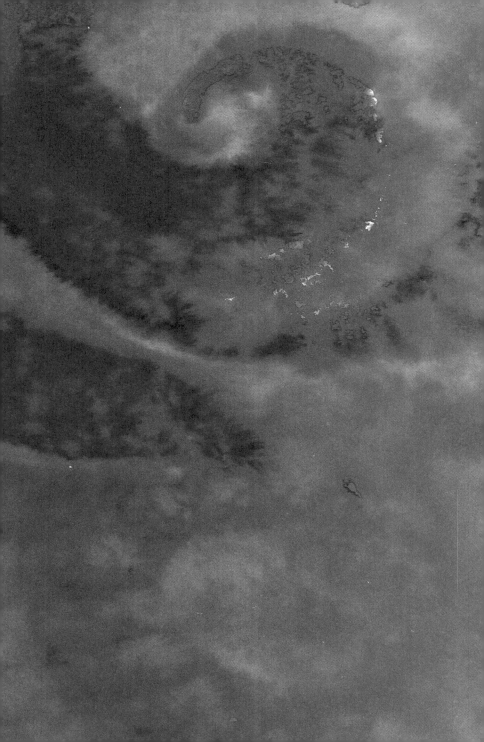

Listen closely, listen well—
It's such a glorious tale to tell,
A tale of heaven and of earth,
How all creation had its birth.

Darkness covered everywhere.
Waters churned and thundered there.
And yet, God's Spirit hovered low,
God's mighty Spirit, long ago

"It is *dark!*"

Then God spoke. "Let there be light."
There was—and it was very bright.
It shone as no sun ever could.
And God saw that the light was good.

Next, to set the pattern right,
God made light day and darkness, night.
And so it happened, just that way.
Time began, the world's first day.

"Oh, my!"

Then God split the waters, so
Some went above and some below.
And in between God put a space
To keep the waters in their place.

Since everything God does is good,
The waters stayed there where they
should.
The space between God called the sky.
And so the second day went by.

"I like the sky."

To the waters down below,
God said, "Now, together flow.
In between I want dry land,
Good rich earth and gritty sand."

Into seas the water fled,
Each content with its own bed.
Dry land stretched out in between,
Swept by wind, all fresh and clean.

"What a
spic-and-span
world!"

Now," said God, "I want some green.
Spring up, grass. You trees, be seen.
Bushes, herbs, and flowers grow.
Color all My land below."

Up sprang plants, quick as you please:
Roses, cactus, lemon trees,
Honeysuckle, mint, and bay—
These and more on that third day.

"Mmm, honeysuckle."

Next," said God, "I think that I
Will hang some lights up in My sky.
They'll separate the day and night
And mark the seasons in their flight.

"Let them be." God spoke the word.
Sun and moon and stars all heard
And rushed to shine at His command,
By day, by night, on sea and land.

"Lights are good."

Sun would rule throughout the days
And bless the earth with golden rays,
While moon would glow as sun would
    cease,
To keep the sleeping earth in peace.

But merry stars just had to raise
A sparkling song of thanks and praise
To Him who set them on their way.
And so it passed, that bright fourth day.

Still, the seas seemed rather bare.
And so, thought God, so did the air.
They should be full. They should be rife
With life, thought God. With life, with life!

God said, "Let the waters bring
Every lovely swimming thing.
Let the birds fly in the air,"
God said, and they all were there.

"It's me! I'm created!"

Whale and shark with sleepless eye,
Dolphins leaping glad and high,
Manatee and seahorse too—
Now God had a watery zoo.

Then the sky with birdsong rang.
Sparrows, larks, and finches sang.
"Fill the seas and fill the sky,"
God said, and day five went by.

"This is incredible!"

God looked next upon the ground.
"I want creatures all around.
On My earth I want to find
Living creatures, every kind.

"Things that walk and things that creep,
Things that mostly stay asleep,
Tame things, wild things, running free—
Let them be now. Let them be!"

And, of course, the creatures came,
Creatures wild and creatures tame,
Wolves and camels, pigs and bears,
Dogs and tapirs, lambs and hares.

Rhinos squeaked, impalas leapt,
Hairy sloths all smiled and slept,
Tigers chased their tails for fun,
And that day had just begun.

"Hello, Adam! Hello, Eve!"

Then God said, "There's one thing more,
Something I must make before
I'm done creating. They will be
A man and woman, made like Me."

So, with love, the great God who
Had made the world, made people too.
With love, in His own image, He
Made Adam, Eve, and let them be.

"It is good!
It is!"

How they must have stood in awe,
Those people, when at first they saw
The world around them, fresh and new,
And Him, the God who made it too.

"I'm putting it into your care,"
Said God. "There's goodness everywhere,
Enough for all. It's good, I say."
And God was finished, that sixth day.

"I'm so glad God created me!"

On day seven shone the sun.
God could rest. His work was done.
But maybe for a while He stood
And looked and smiled, "It's *very* good."

God put His world into our care,
His earth, His creatures everywhere.
It's such a glorious tale to tell.
Listen closely, listen well.

"Please take care of us too."